The Picnic

Chris Baines
& Penny Ives

FRANCES LINCOLN
WINDWARD

It's a lovely sunny day and everybody is very hungry. Down in the long grass a tiny grub is just finishing off his third leaf of the day. The big shiny beetle is hungry too. Yum yum – a greedy little grub is just the thing for a beetle's dinner.

He's so hungry, he doesn't notice there's a
beady-eyed bird creeping up on him. The big
shiny beetle creeps nearer and nearer to the
greedy little grub and the beady-eyed bird
creeps nearer and nearer to the big shiny
beetle . . .

Suddenly – whoosh!
The beady-eyed bird flies up into the old
apple tree, the shiny beetle dives under
a stone, and the tiny little grub lies
very still. He even stops chewing his
fourth leaf. Something very big and very
noisy is galloping through the long grass
towards them. Whatever can it be?

It's the children! They're feeling hungry too. They're going to have a picnic in the long grass. They've brought some crumbly biscuits, a pot of strawberry-flavoured yoghurt, and a bottle of fizzy pop. But just as the first biscuit dips into the yoghurt, and the first SSSSS of air fizzes out of the pop bottle,

a big black cloud covers the
sun, and it looks like rain.

Suddenly it's pouring with rain! The children grab their rug and rush back home, dropping all their picnic as they go. The biscuits crumble into hundreds of crumbs. The fizzy pop pours out of the bottle – glug glug glug all over the ground. The pot of yoghurt lands in the branches of a spiky bush. What a waste!

Very soon the rain stops and the sun comes out again. The beady-eyed bird flies down from her tree-top. All those crumbs – much tastier than a hard shiny beetle! The butterfly can't eat crumbs but she can drink fizzy pop – especially when it starts to go sticky in the sunshine.

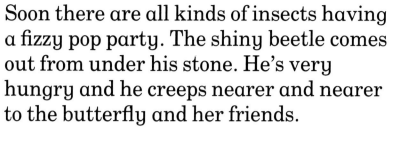

Soon there are all kinds of insects having a fizzy pop party. The shiny beetle comes out from under his stone. He's very hungry and he creeps nearer and nearer to the butterfly and her friends.

The greedy little grub is starting his seventh leaf of the day. The fizzy pop party is in full swing. The shiny beetle just can't wait any longer. He rushes out of the long grass – but the butterfly and her friends see him coming. As they fly up into the air the beetle makes a grab for the butterfly, but he misses, and slips down inside the neck of the empty pop bottle. He's trapped.

The yoghurt drips and dribbles over the edge of the yoghurt pot, all over the crumbly biscuit crumbs down below. The beady-eyed bird pecks and pecks until every one of the yoghurt-flavoured crumbly biscuit crumbs has been gobbled up. She's still hungry, and she tries to eat the yoghurt that's left inside the pot, but it's very sticky and she gets it all over her beak and feathers – what a mess! As she flies back up into the tree, she knocks the yoghurt pot out of the bush and down onto the ground.

A slug slides out from its hole under a stone and starts to look for food. What's this? A puddle of lovely sticky yoghurt. Just the thing for a starving slug! In no time at all there are lots of slugs, all having their own picnic in the long grass and slurping up the yoghurt. They don't stop eating until the yoghurt puddle is dry, and the yoghurt pot is completely clean – not a drop of yoghurt left.

The slugs are very full after their picnic. They wobble like little fat jellies as they slide out of the yoghurt pot – but guess who's spotted them The beady-eyed bird swoops down from her tree top. She can still remember the delicious taste of crumbly biscuit crumbs covered in yoghurt. What better pudding could there be than a nice juicy slug or two – stuffed full of yoghurt of course – and no need to get her feathers sticky this time.

And what about the greedy little grub?
Well, he's just finished his twelfth leaf
of the day and he's not a greedy *little*
grub any more – he's a very podgy *big*
grub. He's a very happy grub too. He
didn't have any of the yoghurt, or any
of the crumbly biscuit crumbs.